Divorcing a Narcissist: Rebuilding After the Storm

How to rebuild your life in the aftermath of a Narcissist

By Tina Marie Swithin

66 *"If you believe it will work out, you will see opportunities.*

If you believe it won't, you will see obstacles."

– Wayne Dyer

The Fine Print

In *Rebuilding After the Storm*, the author, Tina Swithin is offering her own personal perspectives on the subject matter of personal healing and growth in the aftermath of a high-conflict divorce, or a Category 5 Life Storm. This book is not intended to offer legal, psychological or therapeutic advice nor should it be used for that purpose.

The author is not responsible for personal decisions based on the subject matter contained in this book. You are advised to seek professional assistance in your area of residence with individuals who are qualified to help you through any portions that you find to be difficult, challenging or triggering.

PLEASE NOTE: Narcissistic Personality Disorder affects both males and females. Throughout this book, the author is referencing her experience with her ex-husband but she is no way implying that this issue is isolated to one gender. Tina provides support, advocacy and guidance to both males and females on her blog and through her consulting business. Tina was raised by a single father and has the utmost respect for healthy men and women. Tina is pro-child and does not align with mother's rights groups or father's rights groups.

Contact Information:
Tina Swithin, PO Box 123
San Luis Obispo, California 93406
tina@tinaswithin.com
www.tinaswithin.com

ISBN-13: 978-0692548509 (Custom Universal)
ISBN-10: 0692548505

First printing: October 2015

Aunt Bev

Everyone needs someone in their life to love them unconditionally and for me, that person is you. Thank you for believing in me even when I didn't even believe in myself. Thank you for being my biggest cheerleader.

I am grateful for you every single day.

Glenn

Thank you for making me feel loved, adored and cherished…and for loving my every color. I am grateful for your love and dedication to our big, blended family.

Thank you for being my "happily ever after."

TABLE OF CONTENTS

THE BLUEPRINT

Warning: If you've divorced a narcissist or are divorcing a narcissist, this workbook has the potential to create change and help you rebuild your life. Proceed with an open mind and a hopeful heart. I hope to guide you through the process of rebuilding stronger than ever after a Category 5 Life Storm. Every one of us is as unique as the fingerprints on our hands. Some parts of this book may pour great light into your circumstances and other parts may not. That's okay!

Over the years, I have discovered many fantastic self-help books. However, none of them were focused on helping people rebuild from the ground up after the devastation caused by a diagnosed or suspected Cluster B personality disordered individual (Narcissistic Personality Disorder, Antisocial Personality Disorder or Borderline Personality Disorder). Through my journey of rebuilding, I have developed a blueprint for my own remodel and I have listened intently to what has worked for my friends and clients. *Rebuilding After the Storm* is a culmination of my own personal tools along with those shared with me over the years by warrior moms and dads on the battlefield.

I encourage you to journal as you go through this book. Sometimes change is fast; other times, it can be subtle. Sometimes, you may not even realize it is happening. Looking back through your writing journey allows you to stop and reflect on the leaps, bounds and baby steps that you've taken on your path to healing.

It is important to remember that we each have our own personal timeline for healing. Emotional wounds are just like physical wounds. They require individualized amounts of time for healing. Our emotional wounds affect our heart and our soul. Sit with the pain and feel it to your core. Trying to cover your pain only prolongs the healing and eventually, you will be forced to feel the pain because it does not go away. I have come to discover that the fear of the pain is far worse than the pain itself. I think of life's pains as I do a splinter. It is easier to deal with the pain of releasing the splinter when you first get it rather than letting it fester and become infected. Emotional pain will fester and become infected over time.

While changing your past would require a time machine, you DO have control over how (or if) your past affects your future. You may still be in the devastation stage, and have not yet taken inventory of your own tools. Look down! Some of them never even left your tool belt. First, pay close attention to your self-talk while embarking on this journey to rebuilding. Are your thoughts pessimistic or optimistic? While we all get into a funk from time to time, it is important to remember that your thoughts are powerful tools.

Pessimists view challenges as perpetual, omnipresent and personal. Optimists view challenges as short-lived and they do not internalize the challenges they face. You have the power to change the way you look at everything in life, including the challenges. This requires you to lift your vision....are you ready? All I ask of you is to show up, be present and be vulnerable. Be open to new ideas, listen to your inner voice, do the work even if it is painful and be true to yourself during the process.

 Reflection and Journaling:

Note: Pay attention to the areas marked, **"Reflection and Journaling"** along with the prompts. Be sure to pause and reflect or journal (highly recommended) when prompted. If you have an "ah ha!" moment or a personal breakthrough, put the damn book down and get into your flow! Your own writing is more cathartic that anything I could ever write!

Living in fear is not living. Be easy, patient and kind to yourself on this journey. Let's go create your NEW life!

THE EMPTY LOT

Like many, I associate periods of my life with music and songs. At the end of 2008, I sat on the cold tile floor of my 4,300 square foot mini-mansion staring at the bare walls with tears streaming down my face. I was losing my home, my business and my marriage. My daughters were just babies – one and three-years old.

My husband, Seth, had been committing financial infidelity for years and we were in debt to the deafening tune of 1.6 million dollars. After Seth allowed IRS notices to pile up for over a year, they swooped in and froze our lives. Literally. My world was collapsing around me. According to reports, this was classified as a "Category 5 Life Storm."

To the general public in our very tight-knit community, we were known as the "golden couple." In fact, that description was the actual title of a newspaper article about us in 2004! Back then, I felt like the golden couple. I was still living in a naive fantasy world and believing that Seth was who he claimed to be although more and more doubt was creeping in with each passing year. When things (finances) were good, our marriage was great. When things were bad, I felt like I was on a rickety rollercoaster that was barely staying on the tracks. When things were really bad, I felt as though a madman was at the controls of the rollercoaster.

In 2008, my therapist gave me a label for this madman: Narcissistic Personality Disorder. Around that time, I watched an interview with singer/songwriter, Pink (Music AOL, 2008), talking about her new album titled, "Funhouse," where things appear one way from the outside but nothing is really as it seems. Much of her new album was written about the demise of her marriage and the album's main song, "Funhouse" hit me to my very core.

One of the things that Pink said during the interview was, "When you get in front of a funhouse mirror, you are distorted and don't recognize yourself anymore. You want out of there but you paid to get in!" Looking in the mirror, I no longer recognized myself. My brother commented that I looked like a shell of my former self. I had lost the sparkle that I was known for. I had lost the sparkle that attracted the narcissist to me in the first place. I felt as though I had been chewed up and spit out by life itself. I was desperate and empty. I was married but I had never felt more alone in my life.

As I sat in my empty house in 2008, I didn't think things could possibly get any worse. Pink's lyrics echoed in my head, "*I'm crawling through the doggy door, my key don't fit my lock no more I'll change the drapes, I'll break the plates, I'll find a new place…burn this fucker down*"(LaFace Records, 2008).

I felt like I was being hit from every imaginable direction. As miserable as I was in my marriage to a narcissist, I soon discovered that divorcing a narcissist was an absolute, unequivocal living hell.

In hindsight, I am thankful that I didn't know how bad things were going to get because I would have probably found a big, white flag to wave. As the saying goes, "you don't know how strong you are until being strong is the only choice you have."

I went through various stages of grief and loss while coming to terms with my new reality. The five stages of loss as defined by Elisabeth Kübler-Ross in her book, *On Death and Dying*, are denial and isolation, anger, bargaining, depression and acceptance. I personally swapped education for bargaining and optimism for depression. Once I began educating myself on NPD, there was no room for bargaining in my mind. That would be dancing with the devil himself. I had no room or time for depression and made my mind up that it was not an option. I had two little girls to protect. While I sent out invites for quite a few pity parties, I made sure there was an end time on the party. Then I dusted myself off and equipped myself for battle.

I spent a total of five years on the battlefield of the family court system while acting as my own attorney. I was a single mom trying to maintain my sanity while keeping food on the table, working full-time and attempting to navigate a broken court system that I found daunting and illogical at every turn. I barely slept during this time period and my blood type went from A-negative to espresso-positive. I lived in survival mode.

During my battle, I endured over 30 court dates (hearings and trials), two full custody evaluations, over 600 hours of court prep, documentation and research along with twelve police reports and three child welfare investigations. This period of my life was a series of victories and defeats, highs and lows.

My story is one of perseverance – a ruling in October 2014 gave my family complete peace. As of October 2015, we haven't seen my ex-husband in over a year and he is not even permitted to have phone contact with our daughters. This decision was based solely on emotional abuse which is almost unheard of in the family court system. It took five years to get the court system to understand the person I was dealing with, but they ultimately saw the full picture. Since then and during the battle, I have worked to put the pieces back together.

My personal journey is one that I would not wish on anyone. However, I can look back and see why everything happened the way it did. If my plight inspires someone to keep placing one foot in front of the other, no matter how dark the path may seem, it was all worth it.

I lost everything, and then I rebuilt my life stronger than it ever was before. I feel confident standing in my truth on a firm foundation. I am on a lifelong journey of self-love and self-discovery. Sometimes, the wind of change may blow your house down but it is often in that storm where we find our true purpose and direction in life.

In 2015, I said goodbye to my career in public relations and embarked on my life mission and true purpose as a high-conflict divorce consultant and family court advocate. I have spent my life helping others, but without clear direction. Now, I am fulfilled and love going to work every day. I hear the good, the bad and the ugly but it is the inspirational warrior parents who refuse to give up (and their children) who drive me to continue speaking out and raising awareness on high-conflict divorces and custody battles.

While in the eye of the Category 5 Life Storm, there were times that I could not see the rainbow on the other side of the madness. It was only afterwards, in the calm, that I could see the beauty in the rubble of my life. It was a new beginning; a new chapter opened.

I am honored to share my journey and experiences with you as you rebuild your house. It is my hope that this book will guide you through the process. Sometimes when it feels like the end, it is just the beginning. Love, Tina

" *"Only in the shattering can the rebuilding occur."* –**Barbara Marciniak**

THE FOUNDATION

If you were out house hunting, one thing you would never hear a Realtor say is, "this one is great but it has a cracked, faulty foundation." A cracked foundation leads to a variety of problems – doors may not open and close properly, windows do not work according to their design, cracks will begin appearing in flooring, walls and maybe even in the ceiling. Foundational problems can be a nightmare for a homeowner. While they can be covered and hidden, problems will continue to mount.

Many of us have cracks in our own personal foundations. These range from hairline fractures to gaping cracks that are under extreme pressure and on the verge of imploding. It is important to identify the cracks and determine the severity of each one. The cracks in our foundation can be a result of a variety of factors such as dysfunctional family life, self-esteem issues, lack of personal boundaries, childhood trauma or abuse, rape or sexual assault and relationship abuse of all types (emotional, psychological, physical and sexual). Just like in any recovery process, admitting to and identifying that there is a problem is the first step to healing.

The cracks in my personal foundation

When I was in my early 20's, a therapist, upon careful examination, recognized that not only was my foundation cracked but that my house was barely standing. She asked me to take one year off from dating and commit to working on myself. When I first sat on her couch, the only positive thing that I could offer up about myself had to do with my toes. I had been told that they were cute. My self-esteem was at rock bottom.

That year was one of the best years of my life. I learned to practice self-care which could be as simple as hitting the 'pause button' for a bubble bath and a good book to something more extreme like a solo vacation to a new and unfamiliar locale. During that year, I took many bubble baths and new chances. I even embarked on a five-day long solo vacation which was a huge step for someone with abandonment issues and a fear of going to the movies alone! I look back on that time as one of the most powerful and healing years of my life.

The cracks in my foundation began forming when I was in the womb due to my family of origin. In 1974, I was born to a teenage mother with a mental disorder. My mother abandoned me to my father's care when I was only 6-months old. She was known to disappear for several years at a time throughout my childhood. To say that I had abandonment issues would be a vast understatement. My mom suffered from bipolar disorder but it was only after her death in 2001 to a drug overdose that we discovered her official diagnosis. It was found buried deep in a stack of paperwork in her apartment. I am self-aware enough to realize that my natural instinct is to form friendships with men (less threatening). When I feel myself pulling away from friendships with women, I have to give myself a reality check and listen to my inner voice. Labeling these issues was critical for me. Over time, a good therapist, personal work, healthy friendships and a now stable life (and partner), I have worked hard to repair these cracks.

My dad, a very young single father, remarried when I was two-years old and went on to have two more children (my sister and brother). This marriage ended when I was nine-years old and my step-mother, brother and sister packed up and moved two-thousand miles away to California. That sure sprinkled a few more abandonment issues into the equation!

My dad and I followed later that year but our lives had been turned upside down and alcohol soon became my dad's coping mechanism. Because of this and a family history of addiction, I know that my tendency is to attract individuals with drug and alcohol problems. Understandably, I've had to become self-aware in this arena. After three long-term relationships with addicts, I have learned these lessons the hard way. Upward and onward!

I am not perfect. I am constantly learning, evolving and I continue to make mistakes along the way. I embrace mistakes and learn from each one. In my younger years, I admit wholeheartedly to being dishonest and manipulative which I believe came to fruition as a survival mechanism during an extremely dysfunctional childhood. I am truly fortunate to have survived my teenage years. Many who knew me back then would say this is an understatement.

While I never considered myself to be a drug addict, there were times that I did use drugs. I was desperate for attention and wanted to be the life of the party. I was the daredevil amongst my friends and I am thankful to this day that many of their parents embraced me despite the mess of a teenager I was not to mention the bad influence I was on their own children!

As an adult, I have come to learn that integrity is number one. Actions speak much louder than words and despite the mini-tornado that I was in my teen years, I have been told on many occasions that I have a very intriguing naivety about me. I am empathetic, caring and compassionate. I embrace life and I have a positive spirit that has carried me through every trial and tribulation that life has thrown my way.

The narcissist is attracted to individuals who exude the qualities and attributes they lack; honesty, empathy and positivity. They are dark, empty souls. By associating with someone happy and sparkly, they are able to fool people into believing that like attracts like. They are like sponges. Over time, they suck us dry leaving us in a fog that few can understand.

The narcissist hones in on your deepest wounds and becomes your salve and your Band-Aid. They lead you to believe that they would never, could never hurt you. They put you on a pedestal in the beginning only to knock you off with great force. While you are down, they rip off the Band-Aid and leave you bleeding. The narcissist is capable of delivering a crack so deep that many never recover.

My God Story

My foundation lacked an important ingredient: the steel-reinforced structure that was needed to hold everything in place. This can best be described as faith in something greater than my own self. I call it God, you may call it the

Universe…my life was lacking this critical structural component.

I grew up hearing that churches only wanted money from people. My only real experience in church was Easter egg hunts as a child and being invited to youth group a few times as a teenager. At the beginning of my divorce, I was volunteering with the Chamber of Commerce and received notification that they needed ambassadors to attend a ribbon cutting ceremony for a local church. A ribbon cutting at a church? By all accounts, I was an atheist and was not enthusiastic as I drove my car up the hill to the church. I remember meeting the pastor and thinking, *"What a NICE, down-to-Earth guy…not what I imagined a 'pastor' to be."* By the end of the hour, I remember thinking, *"I don't go to church but if I did, this wouldn't be a bad place to be."*

A few nights later, on a Saturday night, I had a very vivid dream. In my dream, people kept approaching me and saying things like, "Ryan Delmore and Ben Daily are trying to get a hold of you…" or, "Ryan Delmore asked for your phone number, do you mind if I pass it along?" I woke up incredibly confused by this dream. More than 15 years prior, I had attended Arroyo Grande High School with both Ben and Ryan. The only thing I knew about them as adults was that Ryan was a Christian singer/songwriter and Ben was the pastor of a church in Texas. I looked at the clock and it was 7am – I felt led to the computer where I found myself Googling, "Service times for Mountainbrook Community Church."

My daughters were only 2 and 4-years old at the time. That morning, I opened their bedroom door and said, "Let's get dressed, girls…we are going to church!" The girls had never even heard the word, "church" before but they got dressed and out the door we went. I dropped the girls off in childcare and walked into the first service. You can imagine the shock on my face when I looked up at the words on the screen and saw the song credit displayed, "Written by Ryan Delmore." The service started and ended with a song by Ryan Delmore. That day, I understood the definition of "God Nudges."

This was the start of my relationship with God. Nine months later, I asked God to come into my life. I originally thought that I would be judged by the staff due to the fact that I was going through a divorce. My experience was quite the opposite.

When I found myself in the local women's shelter with less than $200 to my name, I reached out to the church and felt supported beyond my wildest dreams. The church came together and assisted me financially in obtaining an apartment and re I had groceries and even Christmas my daughters. As a very independent person and active member of the community, this was an incredibly humbling time for me in so many ways.

This experience was the beginning of my God-infused foundation. After taking a class at the church a few years later, I honed in on my spiritual gifts and felt clear in my direction. I turned my small grassroots movement, One Mom's Battle, into a non-profit organization which now has over 100 chapters around the world. While I once feared judgment from the church, I have found only acceptance, unconditional love, encouragement and support. I am thankful for that ribbon cutting ceremony in January 2009 and for the God nudges that have defined my path and my purpose.

❝ *"Grace is meeting those moments on the journey, then picking yourself back up, being humble enough to learn, and not being too hard on yourself."* – **Michelle Peluso**

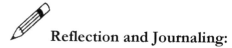 **Reflection and Journaling:**

What are cracks in your foundation? What were the earliest cracks dating back to your childhood? Where else in your life have the cracks formed or spread throughout your home?

Minor cracks, once acknowledged, can be repaired with some elbow grease and TLC. Major cracks can undermine your structural integrity and will require a lot more attention and the assistance of a structural engineer (aka a kick-ass therapist!). In a house, you can ignore or hide a cracked foundation with superficial but temporary repairs. As human beings, we can do the same thing. There are lots of temporary fixes available. However, over time, you will see the cracks begin to spread up the walls (or into your life). A cracked foundation doesn't fix itself! I can't emphasize enough the importance of honestly examining your foundation. If you do not identify the problem areas, how do you move forward in a healthy, stable manner?

Once you've clearly identified the cracks in your foundation, it's important to become aware of these issues and how they spill over into your life. As a survivor of financial infidelity, I am hypersensitive to money issues and I need to be aware of that. I refuse to let my past affect my current relationship. In my case, communication is key. When talk of finances becomes too much,

I need to practice self-care in the form of a mantra to re-center myself. During tax season, my sensitivities are heightened. I may need to remove myself from conversations or take a walk around the block. While talking to a CPA last year (whom I had never met), he asked me to stop and breathe. I had to laugh at the notion that I was doing Lamaze breathing over the phone with a complete stranger! Awareness surrounding your personal weaknesses is critical.

The power of positive thinking: concrete thoughts for your new foundation

It sounds so cliché, but I can't emphasize enough the power of positive thinking. Negative thoughts are fractured, broken and all-consuming. When you are tempted to indulge in thought patterns such as worry or negativity, choose to replace them with solid, concrete thoughts instead. Stop the negative thought in its tracks and make a conscious choice to go another direction. Create a personal mantra to repeat to yourself during these times, *"I only use solid, concrete thoughts."* Just like working out at the gym or developing a new routine, learning to use concrete thoughts will take time. A personal mantra that I use is: "Breathe in positive...breathe out negative" and I repeat this to myself while inhaling and exhaling.

Reflection and Journaling:

What will your personal mantra be? Create the most concrete, positive manta that will re-center you when you need it most. Your mantra is like a reset button when negative thoughts threaten to create stormy skies and thunder.

My go-to mantra is:

_____

_____

_____

Examine your thoughts at this junction in your life?

Are you feeling stuck? Are you asking yourself, "Why me?" and "Why didn't I do X, Y or Z?" Are those concrete thoughts or is this thought pattern creating additional cracks in your foundation? Why not ask yourself, "What lessons can I learn from this period of my life?" or "What steps can I take to move forward?" You have to learn to recognize the foundation cracking thoughts and stop them in their tracks. Replace them with foundation-strengthening thoughts.

I recently read a powerful quote that inspired me to create a social media movement called, "Tina's

Joy Challenge." The quote was, *"Talking about our problems is our greatest addiction. Talk about your joys instead."* It is so easy to get caught up in complaining and venting while in the midst of a Life Storm. I can't begin to tell you how many times my clients have expressed sadness over lost friendships due to their divorce or custody battle. People grow tired and weary of hearing about a battle that they just cannot grasp.

Make sure to check in with yourself when it comes to your friendships. *Are you dominating the conversation with talk of your divorce?* Talking with friends is encouraged but dominating the friendship is not. Healthy friendships are a give and take so make sure that you are monitoring yourself and not crossing the "venting limits."

After you've identified a problem, ask yourself if you are repeating the problem over and over just to vent or if you are working towards obtaining new views or solutions for the problem. Align with a support group and a therapist who is well versed in high-conflict divorce so that your friends can enjoy the happy, joyous side of you.

When attempting to change thought patterns from negative (worrisome) to positive (joyful), it's important to examine your life as a whole. I am a list person and I am also a big fan of moving thoughts from my brain to paper which allows me to dissect them. Left floating around in your brain, these thoughts will feed off of each other and grow in size.

When you are thinking with your emotional brain (and yes, I am convinced there is such a thing!), things can become overwhelming and you are more likely to overreact to everyday situations. Take a deep breath and summon your rational brain forward!

 Reflection and Journaling:

Grab your pen and paper and list all of the categories in your life such as **health, fitness, career, relationships, free time, relationship with your Higher Power,** etc., and under each category, list the things you are thankful for. Then, list the areas you feel needs a bit of "home improvement." Grab your contractor hat and create an action plan. These are the steps that lead you to forward momentum versus the feeling of being stuck.

My Pastor recently told a story about the foundation of his home being poured many years ago. His family and friends wrote scriptures on small pieces of paper that were then folded into the concrete after it was poured and before it hardened. My vision for your foundation includes faith, love, positive thoughts, hopes and dreams. Remember that the stronger the foundation, the more stable your home will be.

❝❝ *"Worrying is carrying tomorrow's load with today's strength- carrying two days at once. It is moving into tomorrow ahead of time. Worrying doesn't empty tomorrow of its sorrow, it empties today of its strength."* —Corrie ten Boom

THE WALLS

This is a time of self-discovery. When we suffer through years of emotional abuse at the hands of a narcissist, we tend to lose our identity. Many of us were married at such a young age that we never got to figure out who we were to begin with. I see life after the narcissist as blank walls that are ready to be painted and decorated.

This is your life and you get to decide who you are, without someone telling you that your needs are silly or that your ideas are stupid. There is no one to tell you that the sky is purple when you know deep down that it really is blue. This is a time of self-reflection, self-acceptance and rebirth.

One thing that I see far too often is walls being constructed as a protection mechanism. Every house needs walls, but it should not require an industrial-sized ladder and scaffolding for others to reach the top. Once you have been hurt, it is a natural reaction to want to protect yourself. However, isolating yourself and constructing walls around your heart is no way to live! It is a fine balance to remain open while proceeding with caution. With time it gets easier, but it is important to practice awareness on a case-by-case basis.

When I met my (now) husband, Glenn, I had recently created a list detailing the 50 things I wanted in a future partner (aka soulmate checklist) which turned out to be an order form to the Universe. I guess you could call him my mail order husband! In all honestly, I was not looking for romance when we met. I was looking for friendship and I was clear about that from the beginning. I almost went running when someone referred to us as a "cute couple." Had I constructed my walls too high, I would have missed out on an opportunity to meet and develop a friendship with the person who has become my best friend and life partner.

Do you remember when you were a child and adults often asked, "what do you want to be when you grow up?" It's time to figure out who you want to be now. The reset button has been pressed on your life and while change is scary, it can also be exciting.

After building two businesses in a small community, my identity was tied to my ex-husband. After the demise of the golden couple, I was in a complete tailspin. My only plan involved a large suitcase and a one-way ticket away from the community that I fondly called "home."

After a few lovely newspaper reporters decided to write articles spotlighting the end of my world as I knew it, I wanted to hide under the covers with a large stash of Girl Scout cookies and a bottle (or three!) of wine. I didn't run away. I decided to stay and face the music and I'm thankful I did.

That first summer was excruciating. My daughters were only two and four-years old and I had never been away from them for more than a few hours at a time. Suddenly, due to a short-lived nesting agreement with Seth, I found myself couch surfing and in a new place each weekend. I kept myself busy to avoid thinking too much, and that generally involved one-too-many glasses of wine.

In September 2009, my custody battle went from semi-amicable to World War 3. I hit rock bottom (emotionally) while sitting in my local women's shelter. I was in fear for my life and it was the wake-up call that I needed. While that weekend felt like the worst time in my life, it was also the best. Obviously, it took several years for me to look back and see that it was a blessing in disguise. This was the weekend my reset button was pushed and I started my new life. I was finally away from the silent treatment and emotional abuse that I had come to know as "normal."

Finances were incredibly tight. I had left with $178 to my name. No savings account. No retirement fund. No job and no back-up plan. It was a scary time and thankfully, within a few

onths, I did secure a part-time job that allowed
ie to work from home. While the pay was very
low, I needed to begin somewhere and I got my
foot in the door at a job that I kept for almost
four years. I remember shopping for used
furniture and the realization that I didn't have to
ask anyone for permission hit me like a freight
train.

It dawned on me that I was free to stand in my
kitchen and throw glitter confetti or have an
impromptu dance party with my daughters
without the dark cloud of my ex-husband
lingering in the next room. I could paint the walls
of my apartment any color that I chose and no
one would be standing by to criticize me. In the
past, I knew that no matter what color I picked, it
would be wrong. I was free to be happy and I did
not have to alter my mood to fit Seth's ever-
changing state of mind. Even bigger, I was not
responsible for anyone's mood but my own! So
simple, but so freeing!

 Reflection and Journaling:

*Which areas of your post-narcissist life are you most
grateful for?*

*What is on your "Soulmate Checklist?" Describe your
ideal life partner and soulmate.*

Compartmentalize the chaos: Feng Shui

One of my favorite parts of my divorced life was a new practice (and conscious decision) to be in the moment. With court preparation and custody battle chaos swirling all around me, I had to compartmentalize the madness. More often than not, I was in survival mode so the thought of Feng Shui-ing my mind was laughable.

It's easy to second guess everything in life and to overthink every decision. It is even easier when you've been subjected to emotional abuse and control tactics for many years. I learned to practice observing my thoughts. Being mindful and present is important for self-care, as it allows you to be aware of your feelings and needs.

Listening to your inner voice becomes easier when you are in the moment. The inner voice is often shushed when we are too focused on the "would'ves and could'ves" of the past and future. In the beginning, being "in the moment" was a forced practice. I gave myself credit, pats on the back, and praise often. I had to remember that being present in two or three moments per day was better than the way I had been living.

Don't get me wrong… I can be an absolute stress case. After feeling consumed by the never ending paperwork and documentation, a therapist suggested that I think of my case as a project or a part-time job where I mentally clock-in and clock-out. If that felt too daunting, she recommended that I pretend I was handling a friend's custody battle which would allow me to emotionally detach.

That particular practice was life changing for me. I began to actually schedule time into my calendar to work on my case just as I would do for a project. The time that I spent on my case fluctuated depending on what was going on at the time but this new strategy allowed me to stay on top of the paperwork versus procrastinating and putting things off until the last minute. Some weeks, my project took five hours and other weeks, it was five hours per DAY! Regardless, I found that being in control of this project (aka my case) was empowering. That empowerment put me back in the driver's seat.

I have always been one to live life to the fullest and learning to compartmentalize the madness was a critical component to surviving this battle. As fleeting thoughts of chaos or fear crept in, I let them "ghost" through my head – in and out but not welcome to set up residence during my days off from court preparation. If it was a thought that would potentially keep me up at night, I would jot it down in my planner under my next scheduled project day. Over time, this exercise became easier and easier.

" *We spend precious hours fearing the inevitable. It would be wise to use that time adoring our families, cherishing our friends, and living our lives.*" –Maya Angelou

THE DOORS AND WINDOWS (BOUNDARIES)

Boundaries are absolutely essential to living a healthy life. I wish this was something that was taught in school. Based on my cracked foundation, my boundaries were pretty skewed. This made me a prime target for the narcissist. I may as well have had a big bullseye painted right over my heart. I like to think of internal boundaries as the doors and windows to your home. The fence and gate are your external boundaries and can take a bit longer to perfect and cement in stone.

In my first book, I talk a lot about hindsight and the red flag reflections. In my relationship, there were yellow flags, orange flags and the more obvious, red ones. I wanted to believe that Seth was the Prince Charming that he claimed to be. I turned my cheek to the little things in the beginning and continued to look the other way for quite a while. I believe this is because for the first couple of years, the positives outweighed the negatives. Over time, the negatives outweighed the positives… but by that point, I was trapped deep inside of Seth's web.

Boundaries have been an issue for me in most of my relationships dating back to my teenage years.

Maybe it is my desire to be liked and accepted or maybe it is my fear of abandonment. Over the years, my inability to say, "no" has caused issues in my professional life and in my friendships. I know that I am a "fixer" and I often take on more than my fair share of responsibilities.

With time, experience and maturity, I have learned that "no" is a complete sentence. I also developed a personal rule called the "48-hour rule." If something involves a commitment of time or money, I give myself 48-hours to make a decision. To my surprise, I discovered that people actually respected me when I informed them about my rule. I was practicing self-care and *healthy* people not only understand this but are supportive of it. Healthy people demonstrate respect for personal boundaries while toxic people, including narcissists, will see boundaries as a challenge.

My self-awareness reminds me that historically, I have a difficult time with boundaries, so it is an area that I pay special attention to. I have worked to identify and understand my physical, emotional, spiritual and mental limits. If something (or someone) evokes feelings of stress, resentment or discomfort, I know that my boundaries are being compromised. Sometimes I simply pull the curtains shut and other times, I use the deadbolt.

Being self-aware is important and in the beginning, you will need to check in with yourself often. That inner voice is pretty darn smart so be sure to consult with it whenever you are in doubt. If you have a pathological boundary invader in your life, it may be time to evaluate your friendships.

To truly honor yourself and move forward after a dysfunctional relationship, you will need to begin setting boundaries. One of the things that I discovered when the fog cleared was that I had many boundary invaders in my life. I have worked hard to rid my life of people who repeatedly deliver chaos or cross boundaries. Emotional boundaries are the doors and windows to our souls. Setting boundaries is how we practice self-love and stop emotional vampires from sucking us dry.

Every day, I have the honor of talking to amazing men and women who have escaped abusive relationships only to continue being walked on by their attorneys, the court system, friends, and family members. While the abuse may not be as blatant as the abuse suffered at the hands of a narcissist, it is still unacceptable. It's time to stop being a doormat and start laying down boundaries. If you don't have them, the storms will continue to rage around you and they will compromise the integrity of your newly constructed home.

 Reflection and Journaling:

Write about a time you haven't spoken up about a topic that you truly cared about. Did you reprimand yourself afterwards and have regrets about staying silent?

Now, write about a situation where you gave your power away and kicked yourself in hindsight. Take yourself back to those moments and examine your feelings. Fear is generally found at the root of all boundary issues. Fear is not real; it's a product of your thoughts. Danger is real but *fear* is a choice.

What were you afraid of? Did abandonment issues surface? Were you afraid of how you would be viewed or judged for saying, "no"? How would you do things differently if given the opportunity to rewind time?

What are your person boundaries and what subjects are non-negotiable for you?

I think it's very important to be clear on some basic boundaries to start with. For me, lying is a deal breaker. As the saying goes, "Fool me once, shame on you….fool me twice, shame on me." I have a zero tolerance policy for people who lie to me. Friends who constantly speak poorly of others also compromise my personal boundaries. Drama is another big one for me. We all have bumps that come up however, there are people who seem to thrive on drama and chaos and need it to survive. I do not want drama in my life, and therefore, those individuals can find the nearest exit.

 Reflection and Journaling:

I encourage you to begin examining your personal boundaries and be very clear about what is acceptable to you and what is not. Setting boundaries does not mean that you are selfish or unloving. It's quite the opposite actually. Once you are confident in your personal boundaries, you will start to gain confidence setting boundaries in other areas.

If someone is speaking to me in a condescending tone, I now feel comfortable standing up and saying, "You need to change your tone or I will excuse myself from this conversation." When you set a boundary, remember that you do not need to explain yourself nor do you need to defend your decision. Say what you mean and mean what you say. I believe that you can be firm, tactful and direct in the same breath. Repeat yourself if you are met with persistence but do not engage beyond that.

 Reflection and Journaling:

Think of a situation that is currently causing you distress in your life. Is fear keeping you from setting a boundary?

What are some phrases that you would feel comfortable using while creating boundaries in your life? Create a list of canned responses.

Here are a few of mine:

1. No. (it is a complete sentence)
2. I have too much on my plate right now.
3. I don't feel comfortable taking that on right now.
4. Let me think about it over the next few days before I make a commitment.
5. I take my commitments seriously and need to think about it for 48-hours before making a decision.
6. That won't work for me.
7. I don't have the capacity to book anything else this month.
8. I don't take client calls on the weekends but I am happy to schedule you next week.

9. I appreciate your offer but the timing isn't right for me.
10. I have prior plans in place that day.

Did any of those sound mean? Selfish? Uncaring? I sure don't think so! Your turn! What are some canned responses that you'd feel comfortable pulling out as needed? I encourage you to make a list and remember that practice makes perfect!

❝ *"Every woman that has finally figured out her worth, has picked up her suitcases of pride and boarded a flight to freedom, which landed in the valley of change."* –Shannon L. Alder

INTERIOR DECORATING

I often describe "this" group of people as the sorority you never willingly sign up for but once you've been initiated, it's the most amazing group of people you'll ever encounter. Narcissists target people with the very traits that they lack. Their victims are often empathetic, loving, kind, considerate and intelligent. They choose the people who light up a room and make the world a better place. Typically, these individuals give of themselves without asking for anything in return. A selfless partner is a narcissist's dream come true. Loving and caring for and about others isn't a bad thing until you begin sacrificing yourself to make others happy.

I remember feeling emotionally devastated after my marriage ended. I was completely drained and in a deep fog. It took months for that fog to begin to lift. It was critical for me to practice self-love and self-care during this time. I like the analogy of the oxygen mask on an airplane. We are instructed to secure our own oxygen mask before assisting others (including our own children). This is an important lesson for our own lives. You have to take care of yourself first even if you have children depending on you. *Especially* if you have children depending on you!

Earlier I talked about the year I took a one-year hiatus from dating to work on myself. I learned to treat myself the way I want others to treat me. Sounds so cliché, I know. Sadly, it's become such an overused phrase, "practice self-love." Just like date-night is important to healthy marriages and oil changes are important for your car, dating *yourself* is important to your soul.

 Reflection and Journaling:

What are the things you used to enjoy doing?

What makes YOU feel sparkly inside? Art? Horseback riding? Reading books? A walk on the beach? Running? A spa day? Meditation? Playing piano? Solitude? There are no wrong answers here. Find the activities that bring you joy and up your dosage! Make a list of all the things that bring you to life and make time for these activities in your planner...in pen, not pencil.

It's been said a million times but it bears repeating: you HAVE to love yourself before you can truly love another soul. Your self-love barometer affects who you choose as a partner, for your friendships, how you cope with life's storms and how you present at your job. You cannot buy self-love in a book nor does it come in a bottle. You cannot borrow it and someone

cannot give it to you. Loving yourself is
something that you have to work toward.

How do you start loving yourself?

This is my recipe for self-love. While you don't
have to follow it exactly, you can think of it as a
basic recipe. Remove an ingredient if you have
mastered it or include an ingredient that you love,
add a pinch of this and a sprinkle of that. Find
what works for your soul and adjust as needed:

1. **Mindfulness**: Being mindful or "in the
   moment." This is easier said than done, I
   know. My brain does not slow down very
   often. My practice of being mindful
   happened by accident and I'm glad it did!
   One day, a few years ago, I noticed a heart
   shape on a tree branch. I paused and just
   stood there absorbing its beauty. A few
   days later, I saw a heart shaped rock as I
   was walking. I paused to pick it up and
   felt a twinge of gratitude for the subtle
   reminders from God. These "heart
   moments" began to occur more and
   more. I would see a heart shaped cloud
   while walking my daughters to school or a
   heart shaped tomato would greet me while
   grocery shopping. I found that the more I
   slowed down and absorbed the moment,
   more of these moments appeared. Now, I

see hearts all day long. Being mindful and in the moment has been one of the biggest blessings of my life. I feel a strong connection to my inner voice and I am more aware of what I think, feel and want. Being mindful of what I want allows me to act accordingly rather than acting in a way that someone else wants.

2. **Gratitude**: I remember hearing Oprah discuss gratitude journals many years ago. I began the practice of gratitude in my mid-twenties and it has carried me through the darkest times. I keep a running tally in my head all day and night of the things I am grateful for and at this point in my life and it has become a natural part of my day. During life storms, I have to force myself into this practice with a good old-fashioned pen and paper. There were times when all I could muster was, "I am thankful for the sun" or, "I am thankful for my next breath." I have come to discover that it is during the life storms that you need gratitude the most. Gratitude is a non-negotiable for me and has been life changing.

3. **Faith**: I respect the beliefs of everyone in my life. My best friend is an atheist. As long as your beliefs do not harm other people, they are fine in my book! By all accounts, I was also an atheist until the age of 34 years old. During my personal Category 5 Life Storm in 2009, I "accidentally" found God during an incredibly vivid dream. It wasn't instant but once I took that first step, I felt as though something greater was guiding me on my path. Now, I feel as though I have an unexplainable connection to something so much larger than anything on Earth. I have an inner peace that I had never experienced before. I believe that each of us has a special gift in this life – there is something in you that the world needs. Being connected to God (or the Universe) gives me a sense of purpose and direction. When I do not understand why something is happening or when life seems really cruel and unfair, I step forward in my faith and I am comforted to know that I don't need to have all the answers. Sometimes, all I have is my faith and through experience, I have learned that it is all I need.

4. **Self-care**: As discussed earlier, this is an important one. Many of us are caretakers and we put the needs of others above our own needs. The more we show love to ourselves, the more we attract love to ourselves. Nourishing and replenishing your soul actually allows you to serve others in a deeper fashion because there is more "authentic you" to give. Those who understand the importance of self-care make healthier decisions when it comes to nutrition, rest, sabbaticals, boundaries and friendships.

5. **Boundaries**: These are a work in progress for many of us, myself included. Boundaries tie heavily into your self-care, and the importance of practicing healthy boundaries is crucial to a healthy life. You set boundaries because you value your mind, body and spirit. Those in your life who are healthy and loving will respect your boundaries without making you feel guilty or unloved. Check in with yourself often and listen to your inner wisdom when it comes to setting boundaries: are you being true to yourself?

6. **Forgiveness**: I am not going to insist that you forgive the narcissist in your life, so please, keep reading. That is your personal decision and we each have our own path when it comes to forgiveness. We have been taught by virtually every religion under the sun that there is great power in forgiveness. Most studies on forgiveness tout the health benefits of forgiveness from both a mental and physical standpoint. The art of forgiveness is simply letting go of hostility or resentment for a perceived transgression. The act of forgiveness is usually preceded by an admission of wrongdoing or an acknowledgement of the offense and many times, a request for forgiveness. I have never struggled with forgiveness until I divorced a narcissist. A narcissist will never admit an indiscretion, nor are they capable of accepting responsibility, which leaves the offended party in an interesting predicament. I believe that the key to forgiveness is that the said offense is in the past. Anyone who has attempted to co-parent with a narcissist knows that the offenses repeat weekly and in many cases, involve the children. I have personally experienced the power of

forgiveness but not in the way that you might expect. I have spent a great deal of time digging deep to understand why I fell prey to a narcissist in the first place. I owned my role in the equation and I acknowledged the yellow, orange and red flags that I chose to ignore during our courtship. Then, I extended an olive branch and forgave myself. The healing that I experienced from forgiving myself was incredibly powerful.

My personal approach to forgiveness as it relates to my ex-husband involves acceptance, rather than forgiveness. I am attempting to shift my perception of the situation by showing empathy for the personality disorder in general. What is life without love and honest relationships? I accept that my ex-husband didn't choose to be narcissist. Acceptance of my ex-husband and my high-conflict divorce does not mean that I forgive his behavior and the actions that cause damage to our children.

7. **Releasing Guilt**: When speaking to survivors of narcissistic abuse, I find a common thread. Guilt and shame seem to

run rampant in this group. Many survivors feel shame that they had once been a victim because they associate the word, "victim" with the word, "weak." They are often riddled with guilt for a variety of reasons but the ones I most often hear involve the future and finances, the extended family involvement in the chaos and most heartbreaking, the effects of the battle on the children. I encourage you to explore and hone in on the hot buttons for you when it comes to guilt and shame. Each month, I speak to psychologists and therapists who are MY coaching clients. You read that right. Each one of them has said the same thing to me in various forms but the underlying message is, "You can't learn this. You can't learn about Narcissistic Personality Disorder (NPD) in a book or in a lecture. Until you've lived it, you really have no real understanding of NPD." If a trained therapist or psychologist doesn't truly understand NPD until they've personally experienced it, you can now release your feelings of guilt and shame. My coaching clients and the individuals I advocate for come from all walks of life and all types of backgrounds. I have encountered brilliant minds such as doctors, attorneys, biologists and CEOs of large corporations. I have assisted people from happy, intact homes and those from broken families. Until you know and understand NPD at an intimate level, no one is immune to this type of individual.

8. **Your Tribe**: Surrounding yourself with healthy, loving friends and family members is a direct act of self-love. During dark times, it is natural to pull back from friends. However, these are the times you need companionship even more. Being open and vulnerable can strengthen the bond with true friends.

Speaking of true friends, Life Storms sweep some friends away and bring others closer. I strongly believe that people come into your life for a reason, a season, or a lifetime. It is important to stop and take inventory on a regular basis. When I reflect back on my early twenties, I was surrounded by unhealthy people. Some of these people were in my life due to guilt or obligation. I no longer operate from a place of guilt or obligation - just because I am related to someone by blood does not mean they are entitled to be a part of my inner circle. I have no room in my life for boundary violators, drama seekers or emotional vampires. I am one of the most open, welcoming people that you will encounter but I have high personal standards when it comes to my tribe. I give everyone the benefit of the doubt but I watch for red flags in friendships just as I would do in a romantic relationship.

A powerful quote that I reference often because it puts things into perspective is this: "You are the average of the five people you spend the most time with." – Jim Rohn.

9. **Living with Intention**: I believe there is something in YOU that the world needs. We each have our own journey and while that may not be crystal clear to you right now, be open to the God Nudges and the signs along the way. When you are living with purpose, you are kinder to yourself. This kindness leads to acceptance and self-love. If your intention is to live a healthy life, you will make decisions that support this goal. You will celebrate your personal victories and you will feel good

about yourself along the way. Begin to examine and establish your intentions even if they start out very small.

Two years into my custody battle, I decided to start a blog to document my journey. One Mom's Battle was born and in the beginning, my goal was to share my experiences with friends and family. Aside from that, I made one intention crystal clear: if one person reads my blog and feels less alone in their journey, it will all be worth it. My intention was born from my own loneliness and despair. I wanted to save someone from feeling the way I was feeling. Little did I know that this one little intention was setting me on a path which would become my life mission and would give me a sense of purpose that I never believed possible. Today, One Mom's Battle - my little blog - is a non-profit organization with over one hundred chapters in five different countries. I am living with intention and I am fulfilled to my core. While your own life purpose may or may not involve creating a non-profit organization or reaching people in the far corners of the world, it is equally important on a human level. Your intentions, no matter what they are, will lead you to your life mission. It may take 5 months or 5 years but is the timeline is irrelevant. Placing one foot on your path could be the start of something magical and life-altering.

10. **Needs versus Wants**: This is where your inner voice becomes your all-knowing, healthy and responsible best friend that holds your best interest as a top priority. It is important to act on your needs rather than your wants. Self-love is to turn away from the quick fixes in life. Being self-aware and in tune with your needs versus your wants allows you to turn away from the things that may feel good or elicit excitement and run towards the things that help you feel strong, purpose-driven and centered. Staying focused on your needs allow you to break unhealthy patterns of behavior that keep you stuck in the past, cause trouble in your life or pull you off track.

Your home is your castle. Your soul is your core. Decorate every square inch with love, kindness and gratitude. Choose to be a *survivor* and release the victim-mentality. You are worth it!

" *"Plant your own garden and decorate your own soul instead of waiting for someone to bring you flowers. "* -Veronica Shoffstall

THE CHILDREN'S RC

I am not one to sugar coat things: having chilu who are caught in the cross-fire of a high conflict divorce is incredibly difficult. If you are divorcing a diagnosed narcissist or someone with very high narcissistic traits, your children are probably faced with situations that most adults are not even equipped to deal with.

The narcissist views his or her children as possessions or extensions of themselves. The narcissist is incapable of empathy and they are unable to place their child's needs above their own. In a custody battle, the children become pawns in what the narcissist views as a game that he/she is dead-set on winning at all costs.

For these reasons, it is imperative that your child's surroundings be filled peace, love and stability. You cannot control the things that happen during your ex-spouse's parenting time but you have control over what happens during your parenting time. I am a firm believer that regardless of the chaos and dysfunction in a child's life, all it takes is for one stable parent or role model to guide them through the rough patches.

My childhood is enough to make most psychologists cringe and in fact, that has happened a time or two. One particular psychologist heard my life story and asked, "How are you okay? Who was your rock? I don't see anyone survive things like this without a solid, stable role model." My answer: my Aunt Bev.

From birth to present day, my Aunt Bev has been with me every step of the way. For the past thirty years, she has been 2,000 miles away but she has been the one person who has remained a constant in my life. She has been with me through the ups and downs and she isn't afraid to kick me in the ass when I need it. She has shown me an unconditional love that every child and adult should have in their lives. I am the person I am today because of my Aunt Bev's guiding light and influence in my life.

It is difficult to accept the emotional pain being inflicted on your children. During the first few years of my custody battle, I was operating in a state of hypervigilance. In many ways, I feel that I missed out on much of Sarah and Piper's childhood because I was completely consumed with protecting them. Several years into my battle, I discovered that the Serenity Prayer needed to be my mantra:

> *God, grant me the serenity to accept the things I cannot change, the courage to change the things I can, and the wisdom to know the difference.*
> - American theologian, Reinhold Niebuhr

It was my job to show my daughter stability and unconditional love when they were in my care. I had to be their role model and I had to turn much of my anger and sadness over to God. I had to know what was in my control and let go of the things that were out of my control. With that said, I also needed to go to sleep each night knowing that I had done everything in my power to protect them within a very broken system. It is a complicated dance and heart wrenching balance.

When your children are in your care, there are a handful of things that you can do to ensure that they walk this journey with the least amount of battle scars:

- **Modeling**: be a role model to your child. Show them what "healthy" looks like so they have a comparison when they are not with you.

- **Boundaries**: children of narcissists are groomed to repeat the cycle of abuse or to be a victim of abuse. Teach them boundaries by having your own boundaries and respecting theirs.

- **Truth**: in the world of a narcissist, the truth is skewed and distorted. Teach your children that truth is black and white and that their word is their most important asset. Teach them to know their truth and to stand firm in their truth. Model this behavior in your own life.

- **Voice**: when children are in the presence of a narcissist, their voice is not recognized as important. Teach your children that their voice is important and that you are always listening.

- **Feelings**: because a narcissist is incapable of feelings, a child's feelings are not validated unless it is done in a manipulative way. Validate your children's feelings at every opportunity. Share your feelings (age appropriate and not court related) about everyday things (sadness over the neighbor's missing dog, etc).

- **Communication**: keep lines of communication open at all times and listen to every word. I began a routine of doing, "highs, mediums and lows" with my daughters. Each evening, I ask them to share their highs, mediums and lows of the day. Use everyday life examples (bullies on the playground, a rude barista, etc.) to discuss acceptable and unacceptable behaviors. Children will begin to form their own connections to the behavior of their unhealthy parent without you saying a negative word about them.

- **Therapy**: aligning with a therapist who understands NPD (and other personality disorders) is very important for several reasons. A well-trained therapist will provide additional validation to your children and will act as a neutral third party to document things that are concerning.

- **Bucket Books**: At One Mom's Battle, we are huge fans of the "Bucket Books" by Carol McCloud. I highly recommend them if you are attempting to co-parent with an unhealthy, high-conflict person. The most popular title is, "Have You Filled a Bucket Today?" This platform teaches the difference between kind, healthy behavior (aka Bucket Fillers) and mean, unhealthy behavior (aka Bucket Dippers). There are journals and other products available as well.

story of the "Tortoise and the Hare," ort wins the race. The Disneyland sona will not stand the test of time and money does not buy love. While it may take a while for children to realize this, they will have more respect in the long run for the healthy parent who was stable, consistent and loving. They will look back with admiration at the parent who was there during the hours of homework, late-night fevers and parent-teacher conferences. Children thrive with consistency and structure so this is the role that you want to play in your child's life.

Your child needs a strong foundation which requires you to put on your oxygen mask before helping them with theirs. This involves a great deal of self-care and being crystal clear when it comes to the items that are within your control. Make your child's room a place of unconditional love, affection and security regardless of the storm that may still be brewing outside of their window.

❝❞ *"It's easier to build strong children than to repair broken men."* –**Frederick Douglass**

THE CONTROL PANEL

The electrical control panel, also known as a "breaker box," serves as the heart and mind of your home. Each of us have a unique breaker box with switches and wires that are tied to past events while simultaneously controlling our present day actions. Just like a breaker box on a house, there are times when the system becomes overloaded and everything malfunctions or shuts down completely. In human beings, this is often referred to as "being triggered." Triggers can be kicked into action by an internal feeling or emotion or an external event or circumstance.

I once went on record with the court and said something along these lines, "No. He has never hit me nor has he threatened my life. He is far too smart for that. I live in fear for my life because of the way he looks at me. If given the opportunity, I do believe he would kill me." I meant every single word that left my mouth that day. I lived in fear. I jump when someone walks into a room and surprises me. My blood runs cold when I see someone who resembles Seth.

Shortly after my last court date in 2014 when Seth lost all access to the girls, those fears were heightened. While walking downtown with my husband Glenn, I froze. I was convinced that Seth was walking down the next block. I went into a complete panic and mental tailspin. Everything in me wanted to take off sprinting in the opposite direction. As it turns out, it wasn't Seth so I am thankful that the rational side of my brain reasoned with the triggered side of my brain.

Being triggered is something that most survivors of narcissistic abuse have suffered through or sadly, continue to suffer through. Our brains are powerful and create associations based on the events or people who harmed us. With time, my trigger points have eased up, but I would be lying if I said that they were gone completely.

If my husband walks into a room and catches me by surprise, I am known to jump in fear. My poor, sweet mail lady has caught me off guard coming up our walkway and I'm surprised she still delivers our mail based on my startled responses! To anyone who hasn't experienced these types of triggers, I would probably appear mentally unstable! A trigger serves as a type of survival response but if there is no immediate threat of harm, it is something you would probably like to do without!

Are the feelings and emotions warranted? That is a personal question for you to answer but I know the answer in my case is absolutely, without a doubt, my fears of Seth are warranted. Living with the knowledge that someone would kill you if the opportunity presented itself is a terrifying way to live. The knowledge that several of Seth's family members fall into that same category increases my fear tenfold.

I am also triggered when people raise their voices or if they yell. I know this one goes back to childhood situations and my father's bad temper. The first (and only time) Glenn spoke sternly during an argument, I ended up locked in the bathroom crying so hard that I was practically hyperventilating. My emotional brain was triggered, but if I could just bring forth my rational brain for a moment, I'd be able to re-set the breakers and return to full-power mode. Easier said than done when you are in the moment!

In my mind, a male yelling or raising his voice is frightening. I have been keenly aware of this trigger lately during my daughters' soccer games. As it turns out, coaches yell. A lot. For me, this is a safe place to become desensitized to my triggers. My rational brain reassures my triggered brain that I am in a safe environment and that is the best place to deal with a trigger!

 Reflection and Journaling:

The first step to dealing with your triggers is to clearly label them just like you would do a breaker box.

What are the things that overload your system and cause your breaker box to shut down?

Knowing where the problem areas are (thoughts, feelings or events) and then having a "go-to" mantra for when you are triggered is recommended. "I am safe and stronger than my trigger," is one mantra but you can create one that feels right to you. Some triggers can be anticipated and some will catch you off guard. Over time and with lots of loving "self-talk" and mindfulness, your reactions will lessen and eventually, you will begin to feel in control.

My go-to mantra for triggers is:

_____

_____

_____

Examining your triggers when you are in a place of peace and calm is also important to the healing process. Reflect on the original moment of trauma. In my case, my trauma happened over a three year period of time when I lived alone. I kept a can of mace and a hammer under my pillow. I never slept through the night nor did I ever feel rested unless someone was staying with me or I was in a friend's home. I would shoot straight up with every sound. I was consumed by nightmares of Seth chasing me, stalking me and trying to kill me. I operated in a state of hypervigilance and carried a large can of Mace around the house at all times. That period of time took a huge toll on me.

Martha Beck explains that the key to healing is to hold the memory of the original trauma while noticing that "here and now isn't there and then." Martha went on to say that, "The smell of burnt toast doesn't mean your house is burning down. An argument with your partner isn't the abuse you suffered in childhood. Fire, abuse, or any other trauma may still occur, but you are different. You're older, wiser, more capable." Dissect your triggers during times of peace and calm when you are in a good mindset to create action plans for the times you *aren't* feeling peace and calm. With time, you will find that your triggers lose their power.

 Reflection and Journaling:

What are your internal and external triggers? What is happening? How are you feeling? What thoughts are

present? Are there days during the year (anniversary, holidays or other emotional pitfalls) that you know will be extra difficult?

If so, map them out on your calendar and fill the days before and after with soul-enriching or fun activities.

What are your coping mechanisms? Taking deep breaths? Mindfulness? Loving self-talk? Reaching out to a loved one? Sound therapy? A long walk?

Remember that the more strategies that you have in place, the more equipped you are to deal with a complete system overload, also known as a trigger.

Please note: Many triggers are so deeply rooted and painful that they should only be explored in the safe, secure environment of a therapist's office.

❝ *"There are wounds that never show on the body but they are deeper and more hurtful than anything that bleeds." -Unknown*

THE ATTIC

In my early twenties, I followed the Grateful
Dead. I was a free spirit who never followed the
rules of the conventional world. An entrepreneur
by nature, I could not imagine being tied down to
a job or having any type of a regimented schedule.
The mere thought of that type of life made my
skin crawl. Initially, my light-hearted, gypsy spirit
was what attracted Seth to me but over time, it
became the thing that he would hold over my
head and taunt me with. According to the story he
created in his head over the years, he saved me
from a certain white-trash fate and demise. My
hero.

After nine-years of conditioning at the hands of a
narcissist, I had been trained in a variety of duties
such as head psychic and mind reader, responsible
for putting out fires and solving all problems
before they even presented themselves. I was
even tasked with predicting the future when it
came to things such as knowing whether or not
the new roof would leak during rainstorms. I was
responsible for Seth's mood swings and knowing
what food he craved even before he knew! I was
the adjuster of shampoo bottles and canned foods
because all labels must face forward, of course. I
was constantly on heightened alert to ensure the
house didn't look like children lived there (gasp!).

I walked on egg shells during my waking hours and I had nightmares about canned food being out of place in the pantry during my sleeping hours. I lived in a constant state of hypervigilance.

This period of my life changed me drastically. It doesn't surprise me when clients get their psych evaluations back and get pegged as emotionally unstable, control freaks. While no one would diagnose me with OCD, I am no longer the free-spirit, Jerry Garcia-following woman that I once was. While I still have an entrepreneurial spirit, I sometimes catch myself second-guessing choices and decisions that would have once come naturally to me. The voice of doubt creeps in and I acknowledge it and let it go as quickly as it came.

I remember one day last year when I realized my husband, Glenn, forgot his cell phone at home. I went into a state of panic. I went through the different scenarios in my head. I could drive his phone 30 miles to his jobsite but what if he was heading home to get it? In my mind, Glenn leaving his phone behind was somehow MY fault and my responsibility to fix. I found myself somewhat paralyzed and unable to think rationally. I was triggered. A few hours later, Glenn came walking up the driveway and I spurted out, "You forgot your phone and I didn't know what to do!" Glenn chuckled and his face said it all. Glenn forgetting his phone was HIS problem. Not mine. Glenn didn't expect me to do anything and he took responsibility for leaving his phone. What a huge weight off my shoulders! Deep breath! Inhale positive. Exhale negative.

Emotional Hoarding

Your attic stores the junk that has been handed down from generation to generation. Maybe your mother was a narcissist who groomed you for dysfunction and chaos in your adult relationships. Maybe you never felt loved or accepted as a child and therefore, you sought relationships with people who kept you in an endless and exhausting cycle of trying to gain approval yet failing every time.

Your attic is also a place to store emotional baggage from past relationships. There could some boxes left behind from your high school boyfriend who dumped you for the head cheerleader on prom night. There may be a few boxes left over from the emotionally unavailable guitarist who strung you along for two years before telling you that he was in love – *with someone else*.

There is a huge portion of the attic dedicated to the boxes of regret and heartbreak over your failed relationship to the narcissist. *A huge portion.*

As we all know, hoarding material items becomes a huge problem and burden over time. Stacks of papers begin to build, things start to smell and eventually, it begins to consume your life. When that type of scenario is occurring and becoming problematic in your own attic (your brain), it's time to take action.

Sorting through the piles

The first step to tackling a job like this is to sort and identify the items you are facing.

 Reflection and Journaling:

Pull out each box stacked in your attic and take a written inventory of the contents. It is helpful to divide the items into piles such as "Childhood," "Relationships," or whatever categories fit for you. Stuffing things into boxes is a quick fix to feel better but pulling them out, labeling them and owning them is the first step to healing and getting rid of the clutter in your head.

While some items may require the help of a professional, others can be dealt with just by identifying them and tossing them into the garbage pile. The story about Glenn's cell phone is a great example of this. I had an innate response to Glenn leaving his phone behind, but once I identified the issue for what it truly was, I labeled it under, "not my responsibility" and dismissed it. While those feelings still come up from time to time, they don't consume me for hours. I acknowledge the feelings, giggle a bit (that came with time) and toss them into the trash pile. Labeling these items means I acknowledge them and own them – they don't own me.

The voices from the past

Attics are the perfect hiding places for spiders, mice and even worse, voices and ghosts from past. I often experience these voices while writing new books or tackling a new project. There are several voices in my attic and the loudest one is the Ghost of Seth. One tells me I am not good enough and other reminds me that I don't have a shiny college degree hanging on my wall. There is the voice of judgment that is critical of each and every word that leaves my mouth. If I feed these voices or allow them to hold space in my attic, they will increase in size and volume. When I wrote my first book, *Divorcing a Narcissist: One Mom's Battle*, I had waves of self-doubt that were almost debilitating. While the book was at print, I could barely eat or sleep. What if I had created all this hype about my book and people hated it? What if?

conversation with these voices goes something like this: *"You are not welcome here nor will I engage you on this matter. You may now pack up and leave."* The voices hiding in your attic can be combatted with ammunition like positive affirmations, journaling and direct conversations – letting them know that they are free to leave your attic (head).

 Reflection and Journaling:

What are the voices in your attic saying to you? Are they questioning your worth? Your career? Your looks or your weight?

Write down all of the negative, hurtful things that the voices are saying and for each one, write a positive replacement thought.

Unpacking Positive Memories

Deepak Chopra discusses multiple studies in *Creating Health: How to Wake Up the Body's Intelligence*, in which participants are able to permeate their body and mind with positive endorphins by focusing on and thinking about happy memories. These are the boxes that you want to bring down from the attic and incorporate into your newly remodeled home.

Focusing on negative thoughts and memories gives power to these moments and keeps us stuck in a victim mentality. In our newly rebuilt home, we are not victims. We are survivors. Anytime your mind starts to take a stroll down memory lane, make sure that you are in control. If you take a wrong turn, simply stop and make the decision to go another direction. Choose happy thoughts over negative ones.

 Reflection and Journaling:

Journal about three of your happiest lifetime memories.

The more details that you can bring forth, the more powerful this exercise will be. Keep your list close and unpack this box whenever the "yuckies" try to rain on your parade. Positive endorphins each day help to keep the yuckies away! Keep your attack clean and filled with only the good memories from your past.

The Future is so Bright

Another strategy to keep the positive endorphins flowing is to create goals. It's easy to take up residence on the couch when you are feeling down, so let's turn that bus around! Lift your vision above this battle or your current circumstances and start planning for the future.

Reflection and Journaling:

Where do you want to be in one year? Three years? Five years? Ten years?

Make plans for each marker (1, 3, 5 and 10 years) and actually map out in detail what your life will look like if you were to hit the fast-forward button. Not only that, but imagine it even better than you want it to be! Shoot for the moon! Once you have your year markers planned out, create action steps for year one, year three and so on. Be sure to write them on your calendar and hold yourself accountable. Share your goals with friends as an extra accountability incentive.

Humor

In my search to find words that are the opposite of humor, words like sadness, seriousness, unhappiness and depression presented themselves. Humor is a powerful and uplifting weapon to battle the darkest of days. Have you ever seen the 1998 film, Patch Adams? In it, patients who were hospitalized but given the opportunity to laugh, even for a few moments, experienced pain relief and strength despite their illnesses or injuries. It can be difficult to find humor in the aftermath of a Narcissist but it is a critical component to healing, finding relief and taking your power back.

I used humor when I began decoding the emails sent to me by my Narcissistic ex-husband. Coined, "The Narc Decoder," in my books, *Divorcing a Narcissist: One Mom's Battle* and *Divorcing a Narcissist: Advice from the Battlefield*, this imaginary device came out when I needed to process the abusive, attacking emails that seemed to fill my email inbox on a daily basis. I could either continue to turn my power over to my ex-husband each time I buckled to my knees while reading his demoralizing emails, or I could decode them to find the absurdity and humor in each bizarre piece of communication. It took a while but the latter option proved to be powerful and healing.

Humor is shown to lower blood pressure, boost the immune system along with combatting anxiety, anger and stress. The Narc Decoder put a funny spin on an incredibly dark time in my life and I credit this little machine for the sanity that I maintained through my personal journey. It is difficult to find humor in the darkness of narcissism so I encourage you to borrow my Narc Decoder whenever you need it.

Here is one example of a decoded email to get you started:

<u>Original:</u>

Dear Margaret,

As you can see, Judge Robinson denied my ex parte request without giving it due consideration. I believe that if she would have had ample time on her calendar to review the documents, she would have clearly honored my request to reinstate visits with Annabelle.

I am sorry that there was miscommunication [sic] last month when I kept Annabelle in New York for an extra week. Obviously, the court orders were vague enough that I truly believed I was in the right.

In an effort to ensure that Annabelle knows she is loved by her daddy, I hope you will agree to let me have a visit monitored by my mother or girlfriend, Candace. I hope you will agree that professionally supervised visits are not needed and having a stranger present will only cause unease and anxiety in Annabelle. Can we please agree to work this out between us versus wasting the courts [sic] time.

Sincerely, John

<u>Processed through the Narc Decoder:</u>

Dear Margaret-

Doesn't it sound sweet when I call you, "D
That's for the court's benefit only. Please do
used to this type of language because as soon as
court is behind us, I will return to calling you
every name in the book.

As I believe you noticed, Judge Robinson
obviously doesn't think I am as important as I
think I am and treated our case like she does the
others. Doesn't she know how much money my
parents have?!

I am sorry that in a very planned attempt to cause
you concern and terrorize our young daughter, I
took her out of state without leaving an itinerary
and without notifying you. I am also sorry that I
kept her a week longer than I was supposed to
which caused you extreme distress and wasted the
time of law enforcement agencies in two states.
Actually, I am NOT sorry…I'm just sorry I got
caught!

To benefit ME, I will agree to have my mommy
or my girlfriend-of-the-month monitor the visits so
they can lie to the court for me. Won't you please
agree to do what is in my best interest? As you
know by my actions over the past year,
Annabelle's best interest doesn't even register in
my mind. It's all about me and my need to control
you, hurt you, and win. -- John

More examples of the Narc Decoder can be found in my books or on my blog at One Mom's Battle. The key is to find humor in the emails and take your power back. Be realistic when it comes to your goals for finding humor, obviously, there is no humor when your children are subjected to abuse. Period. There will be emails like the one above which are prime candidates for the Narc Decoder. Make it a game and involve your best friend or your sister. Laughter shared with a loved one is truly the best medicine!

 Reflection and Journaling:

Find a recent email from your ex and process it through the Narc Decoder.

Remember that most narcissistic emails are riddled with projection, deflection, control and the need to win.

Many people believe that when things change, they will be happy. This thought pattern keeps us stuck on square one. When you are happy, things will change. Your views and perceptions of things will change. Open the windows in your attic to feel the warm, healing sunlight and the cool breeze. You are in control of your life and your destiny. No more darkness, cluttered, musty thoughts and feelings. You have the tools and desire to make your attic a happy place filled with positive memories and exciting life goals! The sky is the limit.

❝❝ *"Happiness is an attitude. We either make ourselves miserable, or happy and strong. The amount of work is the same." – Francesca Reigler*

THE GARDEN

Your garden is the place you take people before you let them into your home. It is a place that is evident of the care it is given. A garden requires nurturing and maintenance. It is a place to demonstrate your loveliest qualities and your consistent commitment to your boundaries all at once. A well-kept garden lets observers of your home know that you welcome beauty and sunlight, but will not tolerate weeds or pests. On the other hand, a poorly kept garden lets observers and visitors to your home know that you may have great vision for your yard, but simply did not nourish it to fruition. Weeds abound, and seem welcome right up to your front door.

Coworkers, book club participants, fellow parents at your child's school, teachers, neighbors, friends, family members, social media followers and folks at the grocery store are observing your life, particularly post crisis. It is natural human behavior to develop a curiosity, and it is good human behavior to be empathic and supportive. Tending your boundaries, and maintaining the soil around your newly rebuilt home is essential to growing the loveliest flowers and most delicious fruits and vegetables to enjoy and share with others.

Keeping the weeds at bay is a vital component to keeping your home in good shape. Weeds represent the slippery-slope allowances that are sent our way to constantly test our boundaries. The good news is that by consistently keeping those weeds out, we soon learn to stop them before they start. When they creep in, (and they will absolutely try to creep in) you will have the skills, tools and fluent ability to stop them early in their tracks. Exercising this kind of precision when establishing and enforcing our boundaries requires us to focus on details, maintain self-awareness and firmness in our commitment to our new lives.

The garden's beauty lies in its evidence of healing. Flowers are most fragrant when they are crushed. You, dear reader, were crushed. And then, seeds of beauty were buried deep in the earth as they were expelled. The crushing process seemed to scatter all you had and bury it deep within the ground to never be seen again, just as if they were dead. The scent released by the crushing force was tragic in its sweetness, a sure reminder that beauty was destroyed and all was lost. Then, when

you begin to work the ground, water your soul
and allow just a little light to pour in, you realize
that the seeds were not buried to die, but to create
life anew! Plants that are healthier in soil that has
been well tended, nurtured and healed of
invasions from those with an unwanted presence
spring to life, and in greater number than ever
before. If you are still feeling crushed, inhale the
fragrance and know that it is about to increase by
many.

Tending to a garden requires work. One must lift
heavy bags of soil and compost, dig deep holes
and constantly fight the weed invasions. As an
organic gardener, you will need to protect your
plants from pest invasions with careful precision
that will require you to individually treat each leaf
and stem. The flowers in your garden require you
to pay close attention to potential invaders such
as aphids and grasshoppers. You may not feel the
need to plant an actual garden, but it is a practical
tool to keep your boundaries in check.

 Reflection and Journaling:

Learning to recognize the habits, people, values and priorities in my life was critical to my healing process... and still is.

Make a list of 3 daily habits that you consider healthy, and 3 daily habits you would like to improve. How would your life be different if you stopped doing each of them, one by one?

Take inventory of your relationships. Who do you complain to? Who is person with whom you always seem to talk about the hardships, history hysteria associated with your life storm? Who is the person with whom you share the most gratuitous or positive conversations? How do you feel after talking to each person? How can you avoid the weeds and grow the flowers?

What are your values and priorities? Make a chart with the following categories: Financial, Emotional, Professional, Personal Progress, Parenting, Friendships and Family Relationships and Romantic Partnership.

Then, rate each category with the following guideline.

1. I am surviving. Barely.
2. I am recovering. Slowly.
3. I am stabilizing. Finally.
4. I am thriving. Cautiously.
5. I am succeeding. Firmly!

Which areas do you want to improve? Once you have that list established, you can begin to improve your life in the domains you want to see grow. First, take inventory of how much time you invest into each domain. Then, determine the weaknesses. Your intuition knows the answers to healing and progress. It is time to tune in to that inner voice.

As hard as it may be, it is important that you are real with yourself about how your habits, relationships, values and priorities affect the outcome of your life's domains. Once you empower yourself with this kind of honesty and commitment to improvement, there is no stopping you! Your healing process will be well underway. Tend that garden. Show the world that you have high standards, and will take necessary measures to keep them.

❝ *"Sometimes we have to soak ourselves in the tears and fears of the past to water our future gardens. Wisdom grows not by sitting in peace and solitude, but by confronting the storms of the past, and studying what triggered them so that we can prevent them from happening again." –*Suzy Kassem

HOUSE GUESTS

The first glances around your newly remodeled
home will show a sweeter and more secure place
to rest your soul than ever before. Your walls are
freshly painted, and your carpets are brand new.
The furniture is pristinely dusted and even free of
fingerprints! The window glass is clear with total
transparency. They also open, shut and locked
from the inside, but you feel like you might want
to let in the sweet breeze. In fact, you are
connecting more and more with the outside
world, and you may be ready to let some of it in
again.

Because you have done the work in this book,
you know that you are likely the target of a
narcissist because of your bright light. You are
capable of great empathy, authenticity and depth
in your relationships. You were put on this earth
to form relationships with people. Your
experience with the narcissist left you with a lot
of healing and rebuilding to do, but you are now
well on your way through that journey. Your light
is brighter than ever before. The fragrance of
your healing is evident in the flowers you have
planted in your garden that are now in bloom.
Your life is back on track, or getting there fast.
Your boundaries are firmly set, your tools are at
the ready, organized neatly into their box. You

are beginning to feel that your home is ready to invite others in.

Your table is set with glowing candles and fresh picked flowers from your garden. It may take a while before you are ready to invite someone into your home and into your heart, but you have done the work. Do not let fear stop you! I would rather risk heartbreak by being open to the potential of love than to avoid love completely due to a heart that is closed off and bitter.

In my own personal healing, it was important for me to own my portion of the dysfunctional equation with the narcissist. I pulled out the magnifying glass and white gloves and inspected the dirt and grime closely. Were there red flags that I ignored? Absolutely. It is easy to place all of the blame on the narcissist, but it is also important to self-reflect from a place of honesty. Almost every survivor that I have encountered can look back and see the red flags that they chose to ignore. I reached out to Dr. Craig Malkin, clinical psychologist, instructor in psychology at Harvard Medical School and author of, "Rethinking Narcissism," for a deeper understanding of what happens when we are in the beginning stages of love.

"When we're in love with someone, the judgment centers of the brain become eerily quiet, and it's

*easy to see why narcissists can slip by, red flags
and all, and cozy up to us for a good long while.
Narcissists who run hot and cold are especially
difficult to leave. The ups and downs put you on
what psychologists call a variable-ratio
reinforcement schedule -- the same pattern of
occasional reward that keeps gamblers racing
back to the slot machines.*

*One key to spotting a narcissist is to bring your
judgment centers back online. Pay attention to
feedback from friends, for instance. They're more
apt to see -- and remember -- important red flags
that you miss, precisely because they're not under
the narcissist's spell (I call this 'borrowed
judgment'). Keep a journal of painful moments,
and ask yourself, is your partner working with
you to understand and prevent them? Learn, and
watch out for, some of the hallmarks of
narcissism: Is every mistake he makes, for
example, someone else fault ('externalizing')?
Does she routinely devalue and belittle other
people in her stories? If so, it's only a matter of
time before the disdain or indifference comes your
way."*

 Reflection and Journaling:

Bragging, grandiose thinking and putting others down are just a few of the things that were the red flags for me in the beginning of my relationship with Seth.

What were the red flags that you chose to ignore?

A Table for Two

If I would have closed off my heart and built sky high walls around it, I'd be giving Seth too much power over my life. People often ask me how I trusted again. It was simple: I *chose* to trust again but I took a different approach than I had in the past. I did not rush progress, and I developed a friendship first. I was not looking for validation, nor did I need to be saved. I did not *need* a relationship. I simply sought a healthy friendship. As my friendship with Glenn progressed, I found that his words and actions were in alignment, and that he valued honesty. I found that he respected me and did not rush me or smother me. I enjoyed his company, yet I did not *need* to be with him during every waking hour. I looked forward to the time we spent together but I also valued my own time independent of him.

Inviting someone into your home may take time. When the time feels right, you will know. Use borrowed judgment and pay attention to red flags. Open the windows, but leave the screens in place. Filter the sweet, sunny breeze so that dirt and flies do not make their way into your home. Make sure that words and actions are in alignment. Do not allow sweet, sunny words to distract you from the actions that make you feel that familiar unease. Most importantly, go to the quietest room in your home so that you can pray, meditate and listen intently to your inner voice. I have yet to hear someone say that their inner voice led them astray.

" *"Love yourself. Forgive yourself. Be true to yourself. How you treat yourself sets the standard for how others will treat you." –* **Steve Maraboli**

YOUR NEW BEGINNING

Congratulations on your new home! By definition, a house is a structure or building but a home is where your heart resides. The key to a lifetime of happiness is in knowing the difference between a house and a home. During my childhood and throughout a series of dysfunctional relationships, I was living in a house. Today, I am doing more than living. I am *thriving* in a *home*. My heart is happy and content. My soul is at peace. I am not perfect nor do I have a desire to be perfect; I am a work in progress and I am enjoying the journey.

You will find that with time, your home will settle and minor repairs and tweaks will need to be made. Things may become messy and you will need to mop the floors and dust the furniture but I hope you will also take some time to sit and soak up the sun in your garden. Spring cleaning will need to be done each year because it's an essential part of keeping things on track and orderly but it can also be cleansing and allow you to de-clutter.

You have made a huge investment in your future and it's one that will continue to gain value as you go forward and make improvements. Never stop decorating your home and keep remodeling to your heart's content. This is a lifelong process that

; old – it only gets better. There will be
ıwns along the way, but your
n is getting stronger and more stable by
Don't look back – you aren't going that

Your key fits perfectly into the keyhole and the
welcome mat is out…what are you waiting for?

❝ *"We are all here for some special
reason. Don't be a prisoner of your past.
Become an architect of your future." –Robin
Sharma*

ENDNOTES

Chapter 2

1. Music AOL, 2008
2. LaFace Records, 2008
3. Kübler-Ross, *On Death and Dying*, 1969

Chapter 6

1. Swithin, *One Mom's Battle*, 2011

Chapter 7

1. McCloud, *Have You Filled a Bucket Today*, 2006

Chapter 9

1. Swithin, *Divorcing a Narcissist: One Mom's Battle*, 2012
2. Chopra, *Creating Health: How to Wake Up the Body's Intelligence*, 1991
3. Swithin, *Divorcing a Narcissist: Advice from the Battlefield*, 2014

ABOUT THE AUTHOR

Tina Swithin survived a
Category Five Life Storm
and took shelter by
writing her first book
titled, *"Divorcing a
Narcissist: One Mom's
Battle"* along with
chronicling her journey
on her internationally
recognized blog, *"One
Mom's Battle"* which was turned into a non-profit
organization in 2014. The same year, Tina wrote
her second book, *"Divorcing a Narcissist: Advice from
the Battlefield."* In 2015, Tina left her career in
Public Relations to dedicate her life to Family
Court advocacy and private consultations with
those involved in high-conflict custody battles
and divorces. Tina has also created a private,
secure forum, "The Lemonade Club," for those
fighting to protect their children from personality
disordered individuals.

Tina has chosen to assume the title of survivor
versus victim and has become an advocate for
change in the Family Court System after seeing
the flaws first-hand. Tina believes that the courts
have lost sight of their primary focus, which
should be the best interest of the child and

instead, are focusing too heavily on parental rights. Tina is working to raise awareness of the issues in the Family Court System and to educate the general public on Narcissistic Personality Disorder and other Cluster B Personality Disorders. High conflict divorces are on the rise and the children are suffering unnecessarily due to the lack of education on the front lines—and behind the judicial bench.

In the past, Tina has been awarded honors such as the "Top 20 Professionals Under 40" and the "Top 40 Professionals Under 40" in several regional California newspapers. Tina has appeared on shows such as *"Dr. Carole's Couch"* and on Huff Post LIVE. Tina's work has been featured in outlets such as Glamour Magazine, SF Gate, Examiner, LA Parent Magazine, About.com, Yahoo, Huffington Post and the Washington Times. Both of her books have garnered 5-star ratings with hundreds of reviews on Amazon. In her spare time, Tina writes for the Huffington Post Divorce where she delves into the tricky world of divorcing a narcissist.

Tina Swithin, LLC
PO Box 123, San Luis Obispo, California 93406
Tina@tinaswithin.com

Websites: www.tinaswithin.com

www.onemomsbattle.com
www.thelemonadeclub.com

Made in the USA
San Bernardino, CA
18 June 2016